DRINKING WAS DEFINITELY INVOLVED

CONFLICT AND SCOTCH
BOOK 1

AL DELUISE

ABOUT THESE STORIES

In a bar one night, talking to a friend, I started to tell a story, which I do all the time. Before I even got into the gist of the tale, my friend said, "I believe, drinking was most definitely involved."

Well, he was right, so the following stories will be just that...

FIRST ROUND'S ON ME

An Introduction

When I was young, I wanted to be a writer.

I wrote short stories, poems, even an unpublished novel (*Ballet with the Moon*— hands down best title for a first novel, ever).

That novel sat on the shelf for years, although at one point I found an agent who was so unscrupulous that I'd rather not talk about it *(and she is still out there)*.

Back to the short stories I wrote and tried to get published.

I remember at times having fifteen or twenty copies of my newest story stacked on the table in front of me, each with accompanying cover letter and envelope addressed to various magazines knowing, in my heart, that at least *ONE* would want to publish my work. Always greatly disappointed by the returned letter that said, and I'm paraphrasing now: "*You suck —don't ever send me anything ever again and oh, by the way, I slept with your brother.*"

Maybe not those exact words, but you get the idea.

Somewhere in my house there is a folder this thick (for those not sitting with me as I write, I am holding my thumb and index finger about eight inches apart) where all those letters of rejection still live and talk about me behind my back.

I tell my kids they are lucky to be living in a world where there are so many outlets available to them which allows people to read their stories and essays, or listen to their music. "Not like when I was a kid," I lecture, one cliché away from telling them how I walked ten miles to school in the snow, or how we actually had to get up and change the channel on the TV by hand. Apparently, I grew up during a technological Dust Bowl; if John Steinbeck were alive today, he would most definitely blog about it.

I have three kids, each with their own creative voice. Although, my middle son, now home from college for the summer, communicates through an intricate series of shrugs and grunts, then moves about the house, Godzilla-like, squashing terrified Japanese people under foot in his perpetual search for food (*How terrified Japanese people got into the house in the first place, I'll never know—isn't that why they got the cat?*).

Then, it finally dawned on me; I also live in this wondrous technological age where any failed writer *(me)* can post his work, without hindrance of editor, good conscience, or talent.

This brings us here.

I used to write fiction, telling stories about aliens or ghosts, or ghost-aliens, but eventually progressed to more adult story lines (*no, not* **those** *adult story lines*). Stories where people worked, fell in love, got married, or committed murder (*usually after they got married*). These were stories that, for whatever reason, no one wanted to read. So if fiction isn't my strong suit, then how about real life? Who wouldn't want to read about a balding, overweight, divorced father of three and his adventures? (*That was a rhetorical question—please don't leave*). Here, you will get to know me, my kids, my family, my friends. Hopefully you'll get to like us, and they won't get mad at me if I give away too many of their secrets.

As for the name of this blog, that was a gift given to me years ago by a very good friend of mine. Phil, whose jazz name is *"Blind Dog,"* is the aforementioned Godzilla's godfather. At some point after my separation years ago, during one of our too-numerous-to-count drunken nights of Phil listening to me commiserating about my life, he just shook his head and said, "My God, Al, your life is nothing but conflict and scotch."

Even in the drunken haze where I was currently residing, I knew these words were special. I vowed right then, fist raised to God ala Scarlet O'Hara, that I would "use this somehow!" Sure, not the greatest vow, I grant you that. It can't compete with, "As God as my witness, I shall never go hungry again!" but I was pretty drunk and surprised I even remembered it the next day.

So, here we are.

Welcome to my life.

Welcome to Conflict and Scotch.

First round's on me.

WHAT A NURSE TOLD ME TO DRINK FOR MY HEALTH

I'm going to tell you the world's worst kept secret: I like to drink. That shouldn't be a surprise since my blog is called *Conflict and Scotch* and not *Conflict and Coffee* or *Conflict and A-Nice-Glass-of-Warm-Milk-Just-Before-Bedtime* . It's called *Conflict and Scotch*. The Conflict was born from a marriage *(and a divorce)* and all that goes with that. The scotch found me in a totally unexpected way.

In the mid-eighties, the company I worked for decided they wanted to keep their employees in tip-top condition. With that in mind, they built a fitness center in our building. There were treadmills and Stair Masters and free-weights all designed to keep us from dropping dead at our desks. The only caveat was that in order to join the fitness center, you had to be fit. Therefore, each employee needed to pass a physical.

I'm not talking about a Navy Seals' fitness test, just your basic *"breath in, breath out, turn-your-head-and-cough, let's take your blood pressure"* sort of test.

Apparently for me, even that was a challenge.

A few of my co-workers and I went down to the company

nurses' office; one by one we went in, took the test, then walked out. That was until I went in for my test. A few minutes into it, the nurse walked over and slowly closed the office door; my friends in the waiting room thought I had died.

I was in my mid-to-late twenties and, to put it delicately, I was fat. I was fat and I drank way too much beer and ate way too much pizza (*is that even possible?*). The nurse told me my blood pressure was 160 over 109. To give you an idea of what that meant: 120 over 80 is normal; 160 over 109 is one point away from having leeches attached to my veins.

She told me if I didn't do something soon I would probably have a stroke. I assured her I would exercise and drop a few (*dozen*) pounds. She then added, most emphatically, that I needed to stop drinking. Again I assured her of my intent to get in shape and to get my blood pressure under control.

Like every other overweight, out-of-shape person, I knew what I had to do and, for once, I actually did it. I started running (*well, walk-lumber-jog at first*) and stopped drinking. I was amazed at how quickly the pounds dropped. It was all beer-and-pizza weight and, within a surprisingly short time, I found myself back in the nurse's office.

My blood pressure was perfect.

I was just about to leave when she again emphatically stated that she did not want me drinking alcohol.

As I thought about spending my summer weekends down the shore cold sober she added this:

"However," a dramatic pause, "if you are going to drink, you should drink scotch."

Whoever said our health care system needed to be fixed don't know what they are talking about; to me, it was just fine.

Apparently, the human body can process scotch easier, with less damage than any other alcohol. I tried scotch once at a wedding reception when I was younger (*well, old-enough-to-drink younger*) and to me it had a cold flat taste, cardboard dipped in vinegar.

Then and there I had vowed to never drink scotch again.

I also vowed to remain married till death-do-us-part, so apparently my vows are not worth the air they are written on.

With my future health in mind, I asked my friend Barbara to come with me and we went to a local bar.

With slight trepidation, I ordered a scotch and water. The bartender placed that first glass in front of me not knowing the role he was about to play in my life. I stared down that first glass like I had stared down that broccoli casserole my mother made when I was a boy, and paraphrased her voice in my head: "You will not leave this bar, young man, until you finish all your scotch."

Like a child force-fed castor oil, I screwed up my courage (*and my face*) and finished the first dose. I ordered a second, then a third. By the fourth outing, scotch and I were old friends; I could not remember why we ever parted ways in the first place.

Since then, like old friends, we've had our disagreements, but always ended them over a glass of, well, scotch.

Recently, history repeated itself and people told me I should drink red wine because "*it's good for me.*"

Conflict and Red Wine—nah, I think I'll stick with scotch.

IT'S THE SUMMER OF SEVENTY-NINE

Right now, it's the end of October. Outside my window the leaves have changed, and the nights come quick, so what better time to talk about a shore house my friends and I rented during the summer of nineteen-seventy-nine in Seaside Height, New Jersey?

What amazes me, when I look back at this house, and that we rented it for the entire summer, was the fact that I didn't have a job.

Where the hell did I get the money?

The world may never know.

But, we had a house, less than a block from the beach. There were six of us, but truthfully so many people came and went that summer I couldn't tell who the original renters were.

Note, that while you read this, I don't use anyone's name. There is a simple reason. It's been over forty years since those events, and my memory may juggle the characters and their situations. I'd rather keep them anonymous than get them wrong.

The events are real, the names have been omitted to

protect the innocent *(and me from looking like an asshole)*.

GET A JOB, YOU BUM

Before the summer started, three of us secured jobs in a restaurant on the boardwalk *(The Whistle Stop)*. Truth be told, only one of us actually ever worked there.

A few days into our non-employment, as we were enjoying time on the front porch, we noticed the manager of the restaurant heading toward our house down the street. Like world class athletes, we sprinted from the porch, ran through the house like it was on fire, emerged from the back door, and hurdled the back fence for the gold, and disappeared into the night, never to work *(or not work)* there again.

Speaking of restaurants...

On the boardwalk in Seaside was a pizza place called The Sawmill. It opened at eleven-thirty every day for lunch, had specials like *"two hot dogs and soda for a dollar"* or *"slice and a soda for a dollar"*.

When they rolled up the garage door entrance to open, we were there. Day after day, week after week, we were there, on the boardwalk, waiting to place our orders.

One afternoon, after weeks of this, the garage door cleared open; the owner looked at us, sighed, and asked, "Don't you guys have jobs?"

"Nope," we answered in unison. "Two dogs and a soda, please."

WAR—WHAT IS IT GOOD FOR—ABSOLUTELY NOTHING

Food was not the only commodity we looked to save money on—there was also alcohol.

Morgan David 20/20 is, to be generous, a wine. It is not a wine to be served at dinner, or on a date, or in any social situation. It is a wine that twenty-somethings will drink to get drunk, quickly, if they have no common sense, and very little money. Hence, its nickname:

Mad/Dog 2020.

You have to be creative so that drinking does not become boring (*didn't know that, did you?*).

One afternoon, with novelty glass in hand (*holds a half-gallon of liquid*) filled with Mad/Dog 2020, I played the card game War with another occupant of the house.

Why is this a drinking game?

Simple—you drink every time you lose.

The best part of that is, someone loses on every hand. In fact, sometimes both participants lose on a single hand. Bottom line: both players get very drunk. Why is drinking Mad/Dog 2020 significant in this game? Because by the end of the game, each person not only gets drunk, they get lobotomy level drunk.

Which led to this:

After an afternoon of War, and no longer able to function as an adult, I staggered into the house and went to bed.

To clarify, this house did not have bedrooms. It had one big room with a half-dozen mattresses on the floor. It had curtains for a door, and to land a spot at night it was first come, first served.

I entered the empty room, fell onto the closest mattress, and fell asleep (*passed out*).

Not sure how much time passed, but suddenly a slew of bodies burst through the curtains, landed on the once empty mattresses, and feigned sleep. A few seconds after that, the curtain drew back, and I looked up at a not-too-happy police officer.

The officer said, in a slow, deliberate voice, "I don't care who took it, just put it back."

Silently, he turned and walked away.

After a moment to process what happened, I got up and went outside.

Not sure what their end game was, but for some reason my friends had unplugged and rolled a soda vending machine from the corner deli to the front of our house. Then, to escape discovery, ran into that same house, leaving the vending machine on the sidewalk.

I turned, paraphrased the police officer's words, and said, "I don't care who took it, just put it the *fuck* back!"

IT'S DEFINITELY COMING DOWN

In May of nineteen-seventy-three, NASA launched the space station SKYLAB. After nine years in space, with its orbit decayed, SKYLAB would return to Earth in July of nineteen-seventy-nine. No one knew exactly where it would enter Earth's atmosphere, so people were rightfully nervous.

One Air Force general, to assuage people's concerns, said, "It's definitely coming down."

Well, I know I felt better after hearing that.

We knew we had to do something, and we knew drinking would definitely be involved.

In the nineteen-seventies, Utica Club Beer could be purchased in beer balls (no time for jokes people, please). They held about five gallons, were the size of a medicine ball, made of a frosty white plastic. Day after day we would buy a beer ball, divest it of its contents, and move on to the next. Once a beer ball was empty, a hole was cut in the bottom, the plastic cleaned of any residual beer, then it was given to me. I drew a cartoon face on the front, nothing particular, just whatever came out of my fingers. The general's quote was written on the back, and the process repeated until we had enough, one for each member of the house.

Once completed, we sat on our porch, beers in hand,

happy in the knowledge that if SKYLAB crashed anywhere near Seaside, we were protected with our heads squarely inside our *helmets*.

SO THIS IS CHRISTMAS

After SKYLAB burned and scattered harmlessly into the Indian Ocean (our helmets worked!), we realized a holiday was just around the corner.

What holiday, you ask?

July twenty-fifth, "Half-Way to Christmas" of course.

We bought an artificial Christmas Tree (how someone, in the middle of July, found a Christmas Tree, I don't know), set it up on our front porch and decorated it with empty beer cans and bottles stabbed on each branch.

It was around this time we noticed that entire families who returned to their cars after a day at the beach would cross the street as to not walk directly in front of our house.

On July twenty-fifth we took the tree up to the beach, planted it in the sand, and celebrated Christmas. Not many, if any, put their blankets by our group. In truth, if I saw those people today, I'd think, "*What a bunch of assholes.'*

Yes, we were those assholes.

THE CHURCH OF PERPETUAL SORROW

And through it all, there was Rose.

In hindsight, I feel sorry for Rose. She was our neighbor, lived alone, and was a full-time resident of the town. If I was Rose, I wouldn't be mad at us (we were loud, but not bad); I'd be mad at the idiot landlord who rented the house *to us*.

Rose would sit in a folding chair in front of her house (*no porch*) and talk to us throughout the day.

"A lot of dead soldiers last night," she mentioned one

morning and I honestly didn't know what she meant. Was there a battle? A national emergency with the armed forces?

No.

To Rose, empty beer bottles or cans left on the ground were dead soldiers.

Rose gave us food, but also admonished our actions at times. We were respectful of her, but didn't curtail our actions because of her. Rose saw it all. A group of guys with plastic decorated beer balls on their heads. A Christmas tree with beer bottles as ornaments. Drinking games and dead soldiers. People coming and going all hours of the day and night. Families crossed the street to avoid our house (*and hers, unfortunately, by association*).

It was a long summer for us. Maybe even longer for Rose.

Rose would come out periodically, broom in hand, and sweep the small patch of cement in front of her house. She didn't seem happy (*hopefully not because of us*), so we called her "*St. Rose of the Church of Perpetual Sorrow.*"

Did I mention we were *assholes*?

THE REASON I WAS SPEECHLESS AT WORK

It was the summer of nineteen-eighty-four, the Tuesday after Memorial Day, my first day at a new job. I stood in my boss's office, soaked to the skin, hair matted down on my forehead, shivering and unable to speak.

Why was I soaked?

A thunderstorm raged outside and, being an ill-prepared young man, I did not own an umbrella, let alone a raincoat to protect myself from the elements.

Why was I unable to speak?

Glad you asked.

That summer, my friends and I rented a shore house in Belmar, New Jersey on 16th Avenue, about a half-block from the beach, the upstairs of a two-family house. Incredibly small for the amount of people who rent it, but had a bath-room and a refrigerator filled with beer, so it was perfect.

Being our first year in Belmar, having recently graduated from our summers in Manasquan and Seaside, we were not familiar with the local bars.

That problem was quickly resolved.

That first Sunday afternoon, we walked into a bar that

became our second home. Turns out, we would spend every weekend there, surrounded by like-minded idiots, content to spend those beautiful summer days bathed in floodlights while the smell of stale beer and sweat hovered in the air. I spent the entire summer down the shore and, ironically, never got a tan. I would be paler when the summer was over from the absence of vitamin D, due to my total lack of direct sunlight.

The bar was Mary's Husband's Pub, and turned out to be the greatest bar I have ever been in.

That first Sunday there we moved through the crowd, getting a feel for the place, spotting some familiar faces. The music blared through the speakers; Screwy Louie, the bar's DJ, a small man with bushy hair, aviator sunglasses, clam-digger pants, a perpetual *I don't give a fuck grin*, played the best music I ever heard.

We soon discovered drinks unheard of back home. I was accustomed to shots of whiskey or tequila followed by a swig of beer. Here, however, they had drinks named "apple pie" and "woo-woo."

Turns out, you didn't just order a "woo-woo"—you needed to know the proper way to drink it as well.

To begin, put your index and middle fingers inside the rock glass, thumb on the outside. Lift the glass to your mouth, down the sweet, sticky liquid, and quickly return the glass to the bar. Then, as if it was the most natural thing in the world, stick your fingers in your mouth, suck them clean, pull them out with a "pop." Then, throw your hands into the air, and shout, "Woo-Woo!" (*Don't judge me.*)

At some point in the afternoon, the crowd parted, and several bouncers, clad in their identical red shirts, carried something from the back of the bar. It was several wooden pieces they assembled into what appeared to be a small stage. The music was so loud, it was hard to talk to each other. I turned to a girl next to me and asked, "What is this?" She responded, but I could not make out what she said. I asked again as the bouncers methodically completed their structure. Again, I could not make out what she said. I leaned down and put my ear right by her mouth; she screamed the answer once again.

"Turtle Races!" she shouted, deafening me before she melted back into the crowd.

I turned back to the completed structure and, sure enough, it had several neatly numbered lanes, partitioned by long strips of Plexiglas. The rafters shook when Gary Glitter's Rock and Roll (*Part 2*) blasted from the speakers. Everyone cheered. Turtles appeared, placed in their respective lanes. A barrier kept them from rushing off before the official bell. I did not realize until after this first race (*yes, there were several that day*), but people could bet on a numbered turtle and win shirts, bandannas, even free drinks. Within minutes, the official announcement was made, the barrier was lifted, and the race was on.

The Roman Coliseum had nothing on this place; people screamed and shouted, faces red as poor befuddled reptiles; their feet slipped on the beer and spit that flew from the crowd moved patiently forward. Some patrons lowered their faces, nearly eye-level to a competitor's turtle, and shouted, "Go back, you piece of shit, go back!" Others provided encouraging remarks to their favorite, "Go faster, you piece of shit, go faster!"

It was the most ridiculous thing I had ever seen in my life.

Until the third race.

"What the fuck is wrong with you—move!" I shouted at number three who, for some reason, decided to just sit still and watch the world go by. I screamed and threatened, but he acted as if he didn't understand a word I was saying. Red in the face by the time it was over, my shirt soaked with sweat and beer (*neither of which were necessarily mine*). After several more races the bouncers returned, rewound what they had done earlier, and the individual sections of the racetrack disappeared into the darkness that was the back of the bar.

I never yelled so much, and so loud, at a poor, helpless, defenseless creature (*unless you count watching the latest Vice-Presidential debate*).

That night I went back to the shore house, exhausted, exhilarated, my throat shouted sore and unable to speak.

Two days later, as my new boss walked me through the cubicles, I mimed my introductions to the repeatedly confused looks on my future co-workers' faces. During those introductions, one thought kept going through my mind:

Damn turtles.

THE WORLD'S BEST HOLE-IN-THE-WALL BAR

Everyone had a favorite bar growing up, a place you could go to anytime and you'd be sure some of your friends would be there (*that does make us sound like alcoholics, I know*). For me, that place was Pete's Bar and Grill. Pete's wasn't just a hole-in-the-wall—it was where the other hole-in-the-walls went when they wanted to get drunk.

In other words, it was the greatest bar in the world.

Pete's was always dark, forever encased in a light that was more dusk than dawn. If anything, it could only get darker. A piano in the far left corner of the bar, with a three-colored spotlight above it, was never played. This is, except for Christmas one year—we walked in and some stranger played the piano, the halo of light around him changing from green to yellow to blue. In all the years we went there, that was the only time the piano was played.

A Christmas miracle.

There were two attributes that made Pete's famous. If you mentioned either of them to someone from the area, their response would inevitably be, "Oh, you mean *Pete's?*"

The first thing that set Pete's apart from other bars was

that the walls in one corner were covered with aluminum foil. To this day, Pete's is the only bar, restaurant, kitchen, store, or home that I know of that has ever used aluminum foil as wallpaper. I assumed it was cheap and, if damaged, a quick run to FOOD TOWN to buy a roll of aluminum foil was all you needed. Resourceful, too; in case the kitchen ran out of aluminum foil, they could just peel enough off the wall to wrap up that take out order.

The second thing was a man named Blinky.

No one knew who Blinky was. Local legend was he was an old friend of the owner who had fallen on hard times. Pete let him drink there for free and provided a room for him to sleep at night. We never found out the truth about him, but any night that we went to Pete's, Blinky was there. He sat at the end of the bar, yellow rain slicker and hat. He blinked uncontrollably *(hence the nickname)* while he drank shots and short beers and mumbled to himself at the end of the bar. He was friendly, we'd buy him drinks, but he was an enigma to us, a riddle whose eyes blinked in three-quarter time.

Blinky may have been the oldest person in the bar, but the pendulum swung far the other way. The drinking age, when I was younger, was eighteen. In Pete's world, however, there was no drinking age. It was not uncommon to see kids wearing high school varsity jackets, their graduation year on the sleeve—even if that year was in the future. It didn't matter; if you had money, you could get a drink.

Pete's was far from fancy. There were two beers on tap: Schaefer and Pabst Blue Ribbon *(before it got highbrow and became PBR)*. It was not uncommon when a beer poured from the tap that a few black specs would float just below the glass's surface. Clean taps were not a priority. That was the price you paid to drink at Pete's, but it was well worth it. Sixteen-ounce beers were forty-cents and shots were a dollar and change. And Pete's had its own type of magic. My friend,

Woody, once put $5 on the bar top to pay for his drinks, only to return from the bathroom to find $5.10.

The bartenders were all characters, but my favorite was a tall, lanky man named Robert John. I don't know if John was his middle or last name, we just called him Robert John. He was over six feet tall with crew-cut black hair and Coke-bottle-thick glasses that made his eyes appear surprised whenever he looked at you. One night, as we ordered a round of shots, we told Robert John to pour one for himself, on us.

"No thanks, guys. I'm working."

We insisted, but again he politely turned us down. Finally, from our persistence, he took down a 12-ounce water glass from the shelf, filled it to the top with Sambuca, then drained it down his throat in one spectacular gulp.

"Thanks, guys," he said to us as we sat in stunned silence by this remarkable feat. He turned and went back to work.

Pete's was more of a weekend bar, so during the week it was pretty empty, except for Wednesday night. That was a big night for Pete's. It was the night the Sunshine Biscuit factory over on Journee Mill Road paid their employees and they all went to Pete's to cash their checks. Pete would be there behind the bar with his cash box; he exchanged cash for paychecks knowing full well that he would reap the reward as they eagerly bought beers and shots to celebrate the night.

There was a very pretty woman from the Sunshine crew that always caught my eye. She was older than me, probably in her thirties (*God, where is that time machine?*). She stood out from the rest, not just because she was beautiful, but because she had a beehive hairdo. This was the late 70s, and even though I knew nothing of fashion, I knew Marge Simpson hair went out in the 60s. I never spoke to her, but I can still picture her pretty face beneath that thumb-shaped tower perched precariously upon her head.

Maybe that was the charm and appeal of Pete's. Teenagers

getting their first illicit thrill of underage drinking—20-something friends gathered to make plans for the long night ahead —factory workers, like ghosts from the past, celebrate the spoils of a week well-worked—an old friend that needed comfort and shelter at the end of a hard fought life. All these people could come together and enjoy a beer and good company, sheltered from the harsh, cruel world.

Or maybe it was just that the beer was cheap and we got free shots.

NINETY-NINE BOTTLES OF BEER ON THE WALL (WELL, NINETY-EIGHT, ACTUALLY)

In the seventies and eighties, we owned the Jersey Shore; it was our playground, our education. Manasquan was middle school, Seaside Heights high school, and Belmar our college. Today, watching MTV's Jersey Shore is like watching a girl you were in love with in high school and seeing she married an asshole.

I was in Seaside over the summer, and I felt the end was near when one of the ice cream stands sold chocolate-covered bacon. My nephew, Dante, bought a strip for a dollar.

"I love it," he said.

I fear for our future.

But, then again...

In 1978 a group of us rented a house in Manasquan for a week in July, just a block from the ocean. Of course, we couldn't just go and enjoy the sun; being teenagers and being guys, we decided to have a drinking contest. Whomever drank the most beers by the end of the week would be the winner. There was no trophy, no cash prize; it was just that at the end of the week you retained bragging rights that you drank more beers in seven days than your friends. To make it even classier, you had to save all your beer cans and bottles for the official count. There would be no confusion at the end of seven days who the biggest idiot was.

The shore house we rented actually lent itself to this part of the contest. There were two floors, with no ceiling between them, just wood beams crossed the open air, indicating where the ceiling *should* have been. There was a wooden rail, about chest high, which circled the living room and dining room, and an open, brick fireplace near the staircase. That was my spot; that's where the winning count was going to be enshrined.

To avoid further confusion, we each had to pick a different brand of beer. I chose Tuborg Gold (*truthfully, I don't remember which brand I picked, but Tuborg Gold stands out in my memory, so we'll go with that*). It was Saturday afternoon; we had each picked our corners (*or beams, or rail, or fireplace*).

The rules were set.

Let the games begin.

It was uneventful for the first several days. The beams and rails filled with dead soldiers; the rooms looked like a giant game of RISK, our different colored armies staked-out our own piece of the world. I noticed that my armies grew faster than the others; I was on a record-setting pace (*well, since we never did this before, there were no records to actually pace*).

By Thursday night, I consumed ninety-eight cans of Tuborg Gold beer in a little more than five days, well ahead of my closest competitor, George (*we'll get to him in a minute*).

Around 2 am., early Friday morning (*or late Thursday night, I don't remember—it was dark*) I was asleep (*passed out*) in one of the upstairs bedrooms when my eyes sprang open and, with barely time to spare, I leaped for the window and threw up on the roof of the front porch; God help whoever may have been standing on the sidewalk (*Is that rain?*).

I slumped back down, white-knuckles on the window sill;

a pain stabbed my chest as my heart pounded, trying to break free of my body (*who can blame it*), but within seconds my head was out the window again.

Lather, rinse, repeat.

By now a small crowd gathered both on the sidewalk and in my room (*no one seems to sleep down the shore*). I couldn't breathe, I could barely talk, but I was able to mouth "AM-BU-LANCE," and out the window I went.

A short time later I was in a hospital bed, a saline IV stuck in my arm as the doctor checked my vital signs. Some friends followed to the hospital and waited outside. The doctor, whom I'm sure had much better things to do, left my room and told my friends the news.

"Your friend has had a heart attack," he told them, I hoped in dramatic fashion, then walked away.

Well, you can imagine their stunned silence after being told their 18-year-old friend just had a heart attack. Thank God this was pre-cell phone, or that news would have instantaneously spread throughout the community to all my friends and family, and they would all have been concerned over nothing.

Turns out, I did not have a heart attack.

Sometimes, when there is a great deal of drinking, food becomes secondary; you may forget to eat. You wake up, you drink, you pass out. When we did eat, in order to save money (*for more beer*) we collectively bought chop meat, hot dogs, and rolls and would cook for ourselves. We would fry up hamburgers in a small cast-iron pan in the kitchen. Day after day, we would fry up hamburgers and hot dogs in that pan. Over the course of several days a thick layer of grease appeared and would greet the hamburger or hot dog that was about to be fried (*Come on in, the water's fine!*). No one ever cleaned the pan, so by the fifth day, you couldn't really tell where the hamburger ended and the grease began.

So, no, I didn't have a heart attack.

I had gas.

The next morning, I found myself back at the house, side-lined from competition, with strict orders not to drink, eat greasy foods, or exert myself in any way. I watched, powerless, as George's army of beer cans slowly caught up, then inevitably passed my boys to become the winner of the first (*and only*) Manasquan Beer Drinking and Rushing Al to the Hospital Competition."

George finished with 112 beers consumed. I could have beaten that number in my sleep (*if I wasn't busy throwing up and passing out*).

George will have the record but, much like Roger Maris, there will always be an asterisks by his name.

George won because Al was too much of a lightweight to finish the competition. So fuck you, Al.

JUST WRAP YOURSELF IN PLASTIC AND GO

When you think of kids' sleigh riding, you might picture a Currier & Ives print of children innocently navigating a hill of snow. When we sledded as kids, it was down the middle of the street, any street with the biggest hill. But the real adventure would begin as we neared the end of the ride—there would inevitably be a cross street to worry about. We were low to the ground, shooting out into traffic, trying very hard not to get killed by a car. We lived in the suburbs, not the country; our hills were covered in asphalt.

Being young, we had to find places to sled that were within walking distance.

That all changed when we learned how to drive.

With a driver's license, we could now explore outside of our bubble, go out and find the best place to sled. It was then that sledding became a contact sport—you hit the hill, and the hill hit back. Our favorite spot was called Telegraph Hill, which is behind what was once named The Garden State Arts Center and is now named the PNC Bank Arts Center (*Way to sell out, New Jersey*).

We did have one tradition before each run. In order to

muster enough courage before we faced the hill, we would consume, I consider to this day, the most disgusting, sticky form of alcohol: MOHAWK Black Berry Brandy.

It is the worst, and yet, it miraculously warmed you from toe to head before hitting the snow.

It was a long way down from the top of that hill, and you had to navigate through an army of spruce trees that tried their best to keep you from completing your run. I had seen many friends fly face first into the open arms of a waiting spruce, only to appear on the other side with exposed skin scraped raw and smelling like Christmas.

It was not an even run from top to bottom—the ground rose and fell beneath your body as you sped down the hillside. There were moments where you took flight, only to crash seconds later on the cold, unforgiving ground. That sudden impact with the earth often caused a conventional sled to shatter—there was a broken sled graveyard at the bottom of the hill. Fractured Flexible Flyer sleds littered the ground; their shattered wooden planks, half buried in the snow, formed makeshift headstones for the dreams that died on that hill.

But sometimes, more than just sleds were shattered.

With my brother Joe and his friend Tommy, we braved the hill on a Toboggan. Sitting with our legs entwined, from front to back, we inched ourselves forward until the front of the Toboggan reached its tipping point, and we were off. With speed increased, we hit the first curve in the ice-packed snow and went airborne. With amazing force we hit the ground, accompanied by a rousing thud and our own series of curse words as our backs and butts took the brunt of the attack. Within a few seconds, this would be repeated, only faster and with louder sounds coming from our bodies and the ground. As we neared the bottom of the hill, something horrible happened. With my brother in the front and me in the back, we flew off the side of the Toboggan to our left. Tommy, unfortunately, with his legs entangled around Joe's waist, flew off to the right. His knee was twisted, and quickly swelled up to twice its normal size.

With great difficulty, we got Tommy to the car—seats down so he could extend his too-painful-to-bend (*or watch*) leg—and took him to the hospital. It would be crutches for Tommy for the next few weeks.

The hill had changed the way that we could sled—it was either adapt or die.

For a time after I graduated high school, I worked in the warehouse of a company that sold plastic resin and recycled plastic products. Nothing like loading trucks with dozens of boxes of severed baby doll heads and various disenfranchised body parts. What they also sold were rolls and rolls of plastic pool liner material. They were aqua green, navy blue, some with various patterns depicting waves on the ocean. When the winter came I *"borrowed"* a couple of those rows and headed to the hill.

With box cutter in hand, I would shear off body size sheets of the thick, durable plastic and hand them out to my friends. We no longer needed a sled; we *were* the sled. Blackberry brandy provided both courage and warmth; we would just wrap ourselves up in plastic and go.

Suddenly, the hillside was covered in odd, multi-colored oblong shapes that streaked above the snow. Periodically we would take flight, spin in mid-air, land on our backs, shoulders, heads, wherever the hill wanted us to go; we were helpless to object. I would start my run feet first and end up on my stomach, backwards, with my face in the snow. With no sled to protect me from the ground, I felt every rock and bump that the hill had to offer. But we would make it to the bottom with enough energy to run back up to the top, and do it all over again.

We had adapted—and we had won.

In time, our fascination with the hill faded and we moved on to other things. But every winter I think about sledding on Telegraph Hill with my friends and those disgustingly sweet, thick, sticky bottles of Blackberry Brandy. I know that if I ever tried this today, I would end up at the bottom of that hill, alongside the buried Flexible Fliers, looking up at the triumphant hill that eventually beat me.

That's why I'll never go back—I'll never give it that satisfaction.

A CHRISTMAS TRADITION FROM YEARS AGO

With all the traditions that come with this time of year, there is one in particular that my friends and I have not celebrated since we started having kids and the holidays became all about them (thanks for ruining Christmas, kids). Every year, after the tree in Rockefeller Center went up, we would gather as many of us as we could find and ventured into New York City. Some years we had as many as forty people. Friends of friends added to the crowd. Our tradition was to first go down to Greenwich Village for a few drinks, then uptown to Rockefeller Center to see the tree, fighting the crowds all the way. Afterwards, we would cross over 5th avenue and go into St. Patrick's Cathedral for the pageantry that was Christmas.

That was the plan each year.

However, it didn't always work out that way.

It was December 1990, and just about five months since the birth of our daughter, Amanda. It was also my wife Arlene's birthday (*December 7th*).

Side note: Every December 7th I post on Facebook, *"Today is the anniversary when a horror was unleashed upon the American people – oh, and it's also Pearl Harbor Day."*

Now, back to our show...

She had not been out since the baby was born, so this year we had a particularly large group to see the tree. A lot of her friends from work, who normally were not part of this ensemble, tagged along to celebrate her birthday and her re-emergence to the party scene. She was sorely missed by them, and in a little while, you'll see why.

A dive bar in the village, The Grassroots, was always our first stop on these excursions. It is three steps down from the sidewalk, and when you walked in the first thing you noticed was the low tin-type ceiling. There was a phone booth by the entrance, straight out of a 1940's film-noir movie. A mirror ran the length of the bar, and our doppelgangers marched alongside us as we headed to the back of the room.

We quickly filled the place.

Shortly after our entrance, pitchers of beers and trays of shots covered our tables. The 'Roots" had a great jukebox, and within seconds everyone danced. I danced with one of Arlene's friends, Karen, who smelled incredible. She was tall, and had the greatest pair of legs that went on forever. When I asked her why she smelled so good (*smooth*) she told me her complete morning regiment, which included the perfume called Obsession.

Needless to say, that's what Arlene got for Christmas that year.

Sadly, it did not improve Arlene's height (*or legs*).

After a few Happy Birthday toasts as Arlene grew drunker and louder (*is that possible?*), one of our birthday toasts was answered by a woman's voice that shouted from the other end of the bar, "Hey, it's my birthday, too!"

Another group, from the front of the bar, about half our size and a few years younger (*turns out it was her 21st birthday*), were having their own birthday celebration. A few more rounds later, our two groups merged into one super-drunk celebration. Arlene and her twenty-one-year-old counterpart quickly became friends. Someone pointed out the time, said we should leave to see the tree, but that suggestion was ignored. More drinks, more toasts, more dances with Karen and her amazing scent (*too creepy?*) and many more calls to see the tree (*which were ignored*) followed.

As time went on, Arlene's head sank lower and lower as she had a slurred conversation with her reflection in the bar top. Eventually, we collectively knew it was time to leave so left the bar and hailed cabs for our trip uptown.

Several blocks from Rockefeller Center, with traffic at a crawl, we paid the cab fare and decided to walk the rest of the way. We flagged down as many of our group as we could find, and reconvened on the sidewalk outside of Trump Tower. Sadly, our newfound friends were gone, but we retained much of our original group. Suddenly, we all had to pee. It was like our bladders synced up when we stepped out into the cold December air.

In search of bathrooms, we went into Trump Tower, found an elevator. Then, like circus clowns in a car, we packed ourselves in and hit a random floor number. When the doors opened, we fell out into an entrance way filled with men in tuxedos and women in evening gowns. They turned to look at us as we made our drunken apologies, re-entered the elevator, and were off to another floor.

When the doors opened again, we waited to be sure we would not intrude on some other gala. When the all-clear was evident, we scattered down the hallways looking for bathrooms. I opened a door to find an empty ballroom with a grand piano that stood alone at the end of the room. With my urge to pee gone, I went over and sat down at the piano and started to play. I didn't know how to play that well, so it was just random drunken notes that staggered through the air.

It was magnificent.

Our bladders relieved, we met outside, and then I noticed Arlene. The birthday beers and shots had taken their toll; she wasn't much more than a zombie. I guided her over to a spot on the sidewalk, sat her down.

Immediately, a police officer came over and told me, "You can't leave her there."

I didn't plan on leaving her there, but in hindsight, maybe I should have. I'm sure someone would have found her and gave her a good home on some nice farm in upstate New York.

I pulled Arlene to her feet, but she was useless; her legs were rubber bands. I hoisted her over my shoulder and carried her through the streets. Needless to say, we didn't see the tree that year. The tradition changed after that. Going forward it was see the tree first then *'haul your drunken spouse on your shoulder'* afterward.

I haven't been back to see the tree in quite a few years. It doesn't really matter, though, because I no longer have the upper body strength to carry someone through the streets of New York.

Merry Christmas.

WITH THE ROLLING STONES, TIME WAS NOT ON MY SIDE

I have been to a few concerts in my life, but for some reason, something always went wrong. I once stood on a ledge outside the mezzanine section in Madison Square Garden to watch Bob Seger. I hovered there, my right arm locked around the rail as I listened to the music and tried very hard not to fall to my death into the crowd below. I ended up in that position because I had lost my ticket stub and could not prove to the usher that the person sitting in my seat was not me.

Before the concert even started, all I wanted to do was sell my ticket and stay at Beefsteak Charlie's where they served unlimited beer with dinner (*we had some very long dinners there*).

Another time, I was arrested at an Ian Hunter concert (*twice*). Also, to save myself from being trampled to death, I threw bodies back into a mosh pit at a Violent Femmes / Pogues concert.

Maybe I should have heeded the warning from one of my first concert experiences, and just stayed home and listened to the live albums instead.

In the mid-seventies, my friends and I bought tickets to the see The Rolling Stones—they played with Peter Tosh and Foreigner at JFK stadium (*no longer exists*) in Philadelphia. General admission tickets, it was first-come-first-served seating. The day before the concert, we headed to the stadium. Once there, and with food and alcohol in tow, we staked out a spot on the cement and settled in for the long night before us.

Well into the night, and into the alcohol, I shoved a makeshift pillow under my head and fell asleep (*passed out*). About 3 a.m. I woke up from an incredibly unsound sleep and found my face stuck to the sidewalk. At some point in the night, someone stumbled by and knocked over my fifth of Southern Comfort; it poured like a sweet, sticky river down the right side of my body.

Without a change of clothes, and the complete lack of comfort on the sidewalk, I grabbed my friend Rob's keys and went back to his car to find some much needed sleep. I told myself I would get up early, find my way back to my friends, and go into the concert as planned. As I tried to sleep in the luxury of his two-door red Toyota Celica, I could still hear the thousands of people that filled the parking lot.

When I did wake up in the morning, I knew there weren't crickets chirping, but there might as well have been; the parking lot was empty. The gates had opened early, the throng had entered the stadium, and I was alone.

To this day I don't know how I found my friends, maybe it helps to be tall, but I did. On the field, around the fifty-yard-line, I found a small group of them. Some others had gone up into the stands looking for a place to sit—others wandered off in search of bathrooms and possibly food. As I settled in and waited for the first act, I noticed a sign at the very back of this open-air arena. A large hand-painted white sheet rose above the top of the stadium, higher even than the initials that stamped the facade. It had just two words: OLD BRIDGE (*my home town*). At that moment, I felt like we owned the place.

I couldn't tell you much about Peter Tosh, or even Foreigner for that matter. We were there to see The Stones. At some point in the afternoon, after they had cleared off the opening act's equipment and set-up the drum kit with that famous logo on its face, a helicopter appeared in the sky. The cheers were deafening as it hovered for a bit then disappeared behind the stadium wall. The wait was palpable, but I knew it would be worth it. The Southern Comfort bath, the neck and leg pains from wedging my six-foot-two frame into a four-foot-wide back seat to get some sleep, even the constant pushing and shoving of the crowd would be meaningless once The Stones began to play.

Then, if you blinked, you would have missed it.

They came out with all the energy you would expect of The Stones. Jagger pranced on stage; we shouted our throats raw. After forty-five minutes of pure musical insanity, they left the stage. It was a great first set, and we knew this would be a concert we would never forget.

And we never did, but not for the reasons you'd think.

The cheers stopped as the sound and sight of The Rolling Stones' helicopter lifted into space and disappeared into the clouds.

We were dumbstruck—that was it? At that moment the Southern Comfort bath and the leg-and-neck pains from wedging my six-foot-two frame into a four-foot-wide seat was most definitely *not* worth it.

And then on cue, as if members of the audience were handed a script, they all found the stage directions at the same time; a barrage of bottles rained down from the sky. In a relatively short time, the drum kit was destroyed. The roadies stayed safely backstage as the bottles flew. Some projectiles did not reach their target, so those closest to the stage found themselves in the middle of a war zone.

We stood safely at the fifty-yard-line and watched as the thunderstorm of bottles turned to a drizzle, and eventually stopped. Shattered pieces of glass littered the stage and parts of the field. The crowd lost its energy and began to wander toward the exits. The smell of my sticky t-shirt sauteed in Southern Comfort and sweat was making me nauseous; I just wanted to go home and take a shower. Eventually, my friends gathered together as they staggered in from each part of the stadium and, in no time, we headed home.

As I think about it now, maybe nothing went wrong at these concerts; it's almost forty years later and I'm still talking about it. I mean, I was hanging in the air *over* the crowd at Madison Square Garden, trying not to die and still shouted until I couldn't talk. I was arrested at an Ian Hunter concert, not just once, but twice *(who does that?)*. And in all honesty, throwing those bodies back into that mosh pit while the Pogues played wasn't just to protect myself. It was fun.

In fact, it was more than fun—it was fucking *awesome*.

PUNCH DRUNK LOVE

Before I begin, does anyone know what the Statute of Limitations is for attempted bank robbery?

Never mind, I'll figure it out.

It's tough to point out our flaws, unless you have a blog called *Conflict and Scotch (it's right up there in the title)*. Still, to realize you have a trait but can't seem to control it can be daunting.

My flaw (at least this one) is that I am a very jealous person when I am in a relationship. To be truthful, even when I'm not in a relationship, I'm jealous. I'm sure it has taken its toll over the years, but what I'm about to tell you is probably one of the worst exhibition of that jealousy.

Author's note: *By the end of this post, I come off as the asshole (for good reason).*

My first year away at college, I dated a girl back in my home town. Not to reveal her name, I will call her Sally. Now, just to be clear, I know a woman named Sally since high school, this is not her. (Hello, original Sally, hope all is well).

Anyway, to say Sally and I argued a lot would be an understatement. Nothing over the top, but there was always an annoyance which simmered just below the surface. While I was away at school we'd exchange letters (actual letters! oh, what a glorious time it was) that mostly contained apologies for whatever happened the weekend before. I know it sounds horrible, but I'm sure most of us, if not all of us, can look back and say, "*Yeah, that was not a healthy relationship at all.*"

Now, let's get to the "*incident.*"

Most Saturday nights, my friends and I would go to a bar a few towns over. I'm not naming names or locations—you'll understand why in a minute.

The bar itself was long and narrow, with a small dance floor, some tables, and a spot for the band in the back. On this particular night, Sally and I hardly talked to each other. Don't remember why, could have been anything; maybe I sneezed wrong, but we barely spoke that night.

As my beers increased, from my vantage point, I could see Sally on the dance floor with some guy. In my mind, they danced much closer than I thought appropriate for someone with a boyfriend. I wore jealousy on my face as a mask. A friend of mine, who read that look, grabbed my hand and dragged me to the dance floor.

As we danced, never took my gaze off Sally and her new *friend*. My dance partner tried to talk me off the ledge, but I was planted there.

When the music ended and Sally still talked and laughed with the guy, I had to leave. Went through the crowd and ended up outside to get some air. My friend Tommy (*not his real name*) followed me to the street.

He caught up to me and witnessed as I punched a street sign (*I'm sure it had it coming*).

Tommy, much like my dance partner, tried to get me to calm down.

It didn't work.

Tommy followed me down the street, and witnessed just as I turned to punch a brick wall, which also annoyed me.

Except...

...it wasn't a brick wall I punched.

As my hand went through the glass, from ceiling to ground, the front window of a bank rained down in front of us.

Without hesitation, I turned the corner and ran up the side street, only to stop when I reached the end of the block.

Out of breath, I started to talk to Tommy. Except, he wasn't there.

Ran back to find him, rooted to the sidewalk as he stared at the open wall once filled with glass.

Grabbed his shoulder and pulled him with me to the other end of the block to regroup. It was then I noticed the blood, and realized the palm of my hand gashed open. Took off my t-shirt and wrapped it around my hand to conceal the bleeding. A moment later, I took the dressed hand and shoved it inside my shirt.

A six-foot-two, bloody Napoleon.

Walked around the block, then we went back into the bar.

I sulked in the corner like a wounded bear (*which I guess I was*), until Sally come over and we made up (*for what? not sure*).

Exited the bar, we see to our right two police cars up on the curb and several officers, both in uniform and plain clothes, review the bank situation. Sally smartly pulled us in the opposite direction, my bloody hand still inside my shirt.

This was a time before CCTV cameras; no one ever came after me for the window. As for the gash in my hand, I should have had stitches. Instead, slept with my blood soaked t-shirt wrapped around my hand as it rested on my chest.

The gash healed better than my relationship with Sally; we ended it soon after.

In conclusion, I would love to say I banished the green

monster that lives inside of me, best I can say it is tamed enough that I don't go about punishing innocent inanimate objects with my fists.

Although, I once threw a drunken bar patron through a butcher shop's window, but that's a story for another day.

HOW AN EARACHE SENT ME TO THE HOSPITAL

I tend not to go to the doctor when something is wrong; I will muscle through the pain until it goes away. Do not mistake this for some strong-stoicism; I will complain every minute that the pain is there. It was this anti-stoicism that landed me in the hospital just a few days before my son Alexander's third birthday.

I woke up that morning with an earache; a dull pain throbbed in my left ear, which was now a dark shade of crimson. I downed a few aspirin and went to work with the hope the pain would go away.

It didn't.

For the rest of the day, I downed aspirin and ignored my co-workers' pleas (*demands?*) that I go see a doctor.

"I'll be fine," I muttered between rounds of aspirins and complaints.

That night, my wife Arlene also suggested I go see a doctor, but I deferred her request for my own form of self-medication.

Scotch.

I was sure all that I needed was a good night's sleep, and certain my fifth of DEWARS would provide that for me.

After what happened next, I should really give back my degree in self-help medicine.

Arlene went to bed and, after I completed about a third of my treatment, I was still in pain. I woke Arlene and asked if she had any ideas on how to stop the pain. After she gently (*Ha!*) reminded me that I should have gone to the doctor, Arlene went into the bathroom and came back with a bottle of pills.

"These are painkillers from oral surgery I had a few years ago." She handed me the bottle. "Not sure if they are still good."

She went back to bed, blissfully ignorant of what was about to happen.

Returned to the living room, twisted open the pill container, took out one white pill and swallowed it with a large swig of scotch straight from the bottle (*I had turned into a country western song*). I waited for the pain to cease as I delivered copious amounts of scotch into my system.

Nothing.

I went back to the bottle (*pills, not scotch*) and swallowed a second white pill. After a few more minutes the pain decreased enough that I was able to fall asleep.

I don't know how long I slept, but I was jarred awake by the fact that I could not catch my breath.. Apparently, while I slept, a middleweight boxer crawled inside my chest and was trying to punch his way out.

I was certain I was about to die.

I ran upstairs and shook Arlene awake.

"Call an ambulance!" I shouted between attempts to get air back into my lungs.

I went down into the living room and waited for either

death or the ambulance; at that point I didn't care which one showed up first.

"Call again!" I shouted what might have been only a minute later, but felt like hours.

Just then, red lights painted my living room walls, and looked up just as the EMT entered my house.

Know those moments in movies where an old man (*played by me in this scene*) clutches his chest and mumbles "*my pills*" to whoever is near him? And when the pills are found, and one is placed under his tongue, he miraculously is able to breathe again, and the pain is gone—I never believed that to be true.

You know what? That is exactly what happened to me. The EMT placed a small white pill into my mouth, and in a split-second the pain was gone.

I could breathe again.

Hoped that would be the end of it—it wasn't.

They took me to the hospital, and I was placed in the intensive care unit for three days. I wasn't allowed visitors, except for Arlene. As they went about their business of trying to figure out why this happened, I had to embarrassingly tell them, over and over, that it was probably the painkillers and the scotch.

At the end of three days, a doctor came in and told me, "It was probably the painkillers and the scotch."

My degree in self-help medicine renewed.

When the ambulance took me from my house, I wore a pair of hulk-green sweatpants and a Super Bowl Twenty-Eight (*XXVIII*) t-shirt. For the three days I was there, and with Arlene being the only person allowed to visit me in the intensive care unit, I begged her to bring me a change of clothes.

She never did.

After being told by the doctor that I was going to be released, and to "never do that again," I called Arlene to come and get me. She told me that since she was busy planning Alexander's birthday party she didn't have a lot of time. She told me *"she would meet me outside in the hospital parking lot"* and she wasn't going to come inside because that would *"take too much time."*

This was the first week of January. We were in the middle of a horrific snow and ice storm. Outside, everything was frozen. I sat on my bed in my sweatpants and t-shirt, and waited for a nurse or orderly to come get me with a wheelchair. After a while, an orderly saw me on the bed and told me I was free leave; no wheelchair was necessary. A little confused (*in the movies they always wheel you out*) I headed for the front entrance.

Clad only in said t-shirt and sweatpants, and with my hospital name tag still on my wrist, I walked past the admittance desk and the guard station, and no one stopped me. I felt like Chief in *One Flew Over the Cuckoo's Nest* (*albeit, I hadn't killed anyone or thrown a marble fixture through a window*) and just walked out of the hospital.

Outside, Arlene waited in what I could only assume was a very warm car as she sang along with the radio parked in the furthest corner of the parking garage. When she saw me, she motioned with her hands, and I could see her mouth the words 'Hurry up.' When I finally stepped into the warmth of the car, Arlene sped off and said, "I don't have time for this."

Her concern overwhelmed me.

It's been a long time since then. Last January, Alexander turned thirty. The green sweatpants have long gone missing, but I do still have that Super Bowl t-shirt. One thing always bothered me about my short stay in the hospital:

They never gave me anything for my earache.

NOT YOUR AVERAGE FATHER'S DAY STORY

People tell me I share inappropriate stories with my kids, that I'm supposed to be their father and not their friend. I'm pretty sure the following post falls under the category, *"What the hell did you tell them, Al?"*

It was Father's Day, more than a decade ago, the kids and I decided to do a tour of the Jersey Shore. The plan was to start in Asbury Park, work our way along the coast to Belmar, then end up in Point Pleasant for a late lunch.

In Asbury Park, as we walked the boardwalk, I got excited as we neared Convention Hall. I told the kids to follow me as I serpentine the boardwalk, like Groucho Marx trying to find cell phone service. I finally stopped.

"See this," I pointed to the ground, "this is the exact spot where I was arrested!"

They must have wondered why I smiled.

———

It was 1980, and a large group of friends and I went to Asbury Park to see Ian Hunter at the Convention Hall. We split into two groups—some had tickets closer to the stage, while others had seats in the back of the auditorium. I was upfront, with about six of my friends. I am 6'2", and at this time of my life, I had a group of friends where I was considered the *short* one. All except for my friend Pinhead, who stood about 5'4 but was someone I would want by my side in a fight any day of the week.

As the lights went down and the cheers went up, my friend George, who was a few inches taller than me, stepped up onto his seat. The first few notes of "Slaughter on Tenth Avenue" could be heard, then curtain opened, and out stepped Ian Hunter.

That was the last thing I saw.

To my left, George was pushed down and crashed into the row of people in front of us. He was up in an instant and on his attacker. Within seconds, the two rows were in battle. Fists flew blindly in the air, landing on friend and foe alike. Through the melee, I spotted a sea of yellow-shirted bouncers as they descended on our group. I was pulled toward the side aisle, my shirt nearly torn off. As my arms were being pulled in different directions it took all my strength to keep my right index finger hooked around the finger that was currently trying to gauge my eye out.

Once in the aisle, and with three bouncers on me, I looked up to see the exit door open and a handful of police officers entering the building. I thought, *Great, maybe they could get these assholes off me.* They did, but not in the way I thought—a few seconds later my friends and I were hand-cuffed and we were marched down the boardwalk toward the waiting police cars.

Once at the station we were put in a small, concrete-walled room where the stench of urine not only assaulted our senses, but then pissed on them for good measure. One lone occupant of the room was passed out on the sticky, dark floor.

Once inside, we of course sang the traditional "Nobody Knows the Trouble I've Seen" while my friend John yelled through the door about his Fourth, Fifth, and Nineteenth Amendments' rights (what this had to do with a woman's right to vote I don't know, but he was on a roll).

One by one we were taken from the cell to explain what happened, and one by one we were given tickets with a court date and told we had to appear. Apparently, the bouncers pressed charges against us.

We explained to the police we still had friends back at the concert, so they were generous enough to give us a ride back to Convention Hall.

I found myself back in front of Convention Hall, standing in the exact same spot I would be in years later when I told this story to my kids.

As I stood there, I could hear the muffled voice of Ian Hunter through the walls, and I caught glimpses of the stage whenever the front door opened. Unnoticed, someone stepped next to me.

I heard a voice ask, "What are you doing here?"

I turned to see a small man with a '70s porn mustache. He wore a tan *Member's Only* jacket. I raised my hand to point at the theater, but before I could explain that I was waiting for my friends, he snapped a handcuff to my wrist. Within seconds, I marched back down the boardwalk, hands cuffed behind my back.

Pinhead saw what happened and asked, "What did you do?" I told him I had no idea, and that he should come and get me when the concert was over.

When I walked back into the police station the officer that had just given us a ride back looked at me and laughed.

"Al, what the hell did you do?"

Again, I was at a loss for an explanation. Turns out, porn mustache *Member's Only* man was their Captain. He had witnessed the first arrest and assumed I'd gone back to cause more trouble. I was issued another ticket, for the same court date, except this time it was the Captain that was filing the complaint.

———

A few weeks later we found ourselves in court. My friend John's *(my constitutionally challenged friend)* father hired a lawyer and got his charges dropped. The bouncer that filed the complaint against me never showed up for court, so those charges were dropped. All I had left was to ask pornstache if he would drop the charges as well. After I groveled enough to his satisfaction, he agreed to drop the complaint.

My record was clear. Now, I could honestly answer in future job interviews when asked if I have been convicted of a crime:

"Convicted? No, never."

After I finished the story with the kids, and with their confused looks as to why I would smile when talked about being arrested, we continued our tour of the shore.

Wondering what to do for the next Father's Day, and what stories I can tell.

Perhaps I'll take them down Route Thirty-Five and show them the parking lot where I lost my virginity.

LOVE AND THE DRUNK DIAL

We've all done it. After too many drinks, we find ourselves doing what our sober selves would never do. We make that phone call, to the one person in the world we know we should not be calling, at two in the morning; the infamous drunk dial. It is the one mistake we know in our hearts is a mistake, even as we scroll through our contact list and press send.

I was in love just one time in my life; truly, deeply in love. It was not with the woman I married, nor the numerous high school/college/real life crushes I professed to in my lifetime. It was with a woman whom I met just after I separated from my wife. I met her in a bar. Crazy, what were the odds I would meet the love of my life in a bar? (*Actually, those odds were pretty damn high.*)

I sat there, beer in hand, a woman came up behind me and ordered a drink. I immediately stood and offered her my seat. She thanked me and replied she had a funny story about a bar stool in Las Vegas.

That was it; true love never had a more innocuous conception.

We spoke for a while, exchanged phone numbers, then

kissed her right in the parking lot (*that's not a euphemism—it was an actual parking lot*). As soon as I got home, called the number to be sure she didn't give me the number of the local Pizza Hut (*she didn't*). From that point on, I'd never been happier.

I never met anyone I could talk to so easily, about anything. The first time she told me she loved me it was like I had never heard those words before. I asked her to marry me, she said yes, and we lived happily ever after.

Oh, wait—no we didn't.

As usual, when we realize we don't live in a movie that guarantees us a happy ending with the price of admission, life gets in the way. Prior to our meeting, and as her divorce from her husband was finalized, she decided it was best for her and her children to move back to the Midwest where she was born and raised. For a short time, I considered moving with her, but we both knew in our hearts that would never happen. I could not leave my kids behind.

The only people that think a long distance relationship is possible are people who never tried to be in one. Too much distance, and time, will kill any relationship; ours was no different. After six months of back and forth visits, trying to figure out how to spend time with each other, it came to an end. The logistics of a romantic rendezvous proved too difficult to achieve, and it ended over the phone on a cold February night. Of course we were still friends, and spoke to each other and wrote letters, but it was never enough.

We both moved on, and during the course of our continuing conversations, told each other of the people we dated. Eventually, our phone calls were few and far between. I found when I did call her, it was after a few drinks, and I would bemoan the situation. She would be very supportive, and concerned, but knew it would never work between us.

We tried and we failed.

After not speaking for a while, and after a few drinks (*and then a few more*) I picked up my cell phone and called. It was late at night, and I knew it was a mistake, but I was happy to hear her groggy voice answer the phone.

A smile hello over the phone quickly faded when I heard her say:

"Al, call me back when you are sober."

The phone went dead.

Embarrassed and sad, I knew what a major mistake it was to call.

After that, I never talked to her again.

She did get married again (*thank you, internet*) and I am sure she is happy not to get any more late night drunken phone calls from me.

In fact, I haven't done a drunk dial since then. One reason is that I now know nothing good could ever come from a drunk dial. And another is that there is no one my intoxicated self is longing to call in the wee hours of the night.

I will periodically butt dial someone, however, but only when my ass is drunk.

———

Author's Note: *Since this was written, I did drunk dial another woman.*

It did not end well, but maybe that is a story for another day...

BIRTHDAY SURPRISES OVER THE YEARS

When we hit milestones in our lives, we expect our families to celebrate with us. When I first met my wife, she threw a surprise party for my twenty-seventh birthday. A strange choice, but she pulled it off. Part of the reason it worked is no one had ever thrown me a surprise party before; I never expected it.

Plus, who would ever assume a party for their twenty-seven birthday (*hence, the surprise*)?

Arlene (*future ex-wife*) and I moved in together just six-months after meeting. As my birthday approached, I had no thoughts of a party. So, when my friend Phil (*nicknamed Blind Dog, also the person who named my blog*) came up for a visit, I had no idea there was something in the air. When Phil and I went to get something to eat, his casual comment of, "I know a place just around the corner" did not trigger a flag. I should have thought, *How do you know a place just around the corner you've never been here before?*

Surprise number one pulled off without a hitch.

Jump ahead, the unintended surprise number two for my thirtieth was the weekend of my wedding, and I didn't realize it was my birthday until we went to dinner Monday night. Surprised to see my birth date written above the buffet table at the hotel.

Side Note: *In that one weekend: bought a house, got married, turned thirty (let's get those milestones out of the way).*

On my fortieth *(surprise number three)*, I got a call from one of Arlene's friends asking what I was doing that day.

The red flag? Arlene's friends did not have a habit of calling me. After that, I was taken by my friends on a hodge-podge of tasks that kept me busy until I ended up at a hall. I walked in where dozens of people greeted me, all wearing masks. I had to go around the room and guess who was whom before they would remove their masks *(nothing like Kubrick's* Eyes Wide Shut, *unfortunately)*.

By the end of that day, I was gifted enough scotch to last ten years. Well, ten years if divorce was not just beyond the horizon.

Ten years of scotch, plus divorce, reduces the timeline to about six months.

For my fiftieth *(surprise number four)*, it was a collaboration between Arlene and the woman I dated at the time, neither of which showed up at the party. Although, the masks returned to an *Applebees* in Piscataway, New Jersey.

For my sixtieth *(number five)*, I expected my family, maybe some of Arlene's family, in the back of a restaurant, with Mylar balloons tied to the back of a chair with obligatory old-fart jokes written across their faces.

So, I was truly shocked when I walked into a room full of people from all aspects of my life. Friends from my home-town, some I haven't seen in years. Work friends, both old and new, along with mine and Arlene's family. It was quite the menagerie.

It's a gutsy move to throw a surprise party for someone

who, just weeks before, spent four days in the hospital (*bad side effect of the flu shot*). However, the surprise was complete.

Also, nice to know, my kids and family can lie right to my face without batting an eye; I'll have to rethink all those compliments I've received over the years; maybe I don't look good in that shirt...

The afternoon gathering turned into a late-night party. Afternoon wine turned into evening scotch on the rocks.

We went to a local bar to see a band.

While very drunk, but very much still on my feet, a woman on the other side of the room celebrated her birthday as well. Always the gentleman, I walked over and bought her a drink, which she happily accepted. My thought? This was Kismet. I asked her if she would step outside, so we could talk.

She said yes, and we walked onto the outside deck. Then we just stood there, because I couldn't think of a thing to say. Shrugged my shoulders, silent, then we went back inside.

Also, in my very intoxicated state, I did something that I never, or very rarely, do...

...that's right, I danced.

Well, I danced, jumped, hooted, punched the air, spilled my drink, then punched the air again.

At sixty, I was proud of myself that I lasted until midnight (*maybe not midnight, but it was dark outside and I didn't fall asleep —until, you know, I fell asleep*).

Throughout the party, everyone said, "This is all Arlene's doing, she pulled this whole thing together."

I don't know many ex-wives that would go through all that work to throw such an excellent party for an ex-husband. I thanked her at the party, and I thanked her again in the bar.

And, most surprising, I have not seen any bills from the party show up wedged between our shared expenses— although, I did think it strange when Arlene asked for one-thousand-two-hundred-and-forty-two-dollars to cover my portion of our daughter Amanda's house warming gift.

Well, I'm sure she wouldn't lie to me.

Thanks again to everyone for coming by and celebrating this milestone with me. And, especially, thanks to Arlene (*and the kids*) for pulling off the surprise without killing me (*unless that was her plan all along*).

THE TRUE STORY BEHIND THAT PROFILE PICTURE

One step away from finishing my first online dating profile, I stopped dead in my tracks. I needed to find a photograph that captured the essence of the *comfortable-wearing-a-tuxedo-as-well-as-blue-jeans-ballroom-dancing-skinny-dip-loving-cuddle-crazy-macho-poet* Frankenstein that I created in my dating bio.

No photograph could compete with that.

When I put up my first dating profile, I was in my forties, and asking another person to take my photograph for the website was not something I wanted to do. Not that there is anything wrong with dating profiles, but I would have rather gone into stealth mode, and not told anyone until I had several dates under my belt. Fortunately, for me (*maybe not so much for him*), I had a friend that had recently faced the same dating profile picture dilemma. He told me he had a camera and a place to take pictures (*suddenly my life felt like a very-special episode of* Diff'rent Strokes).

To start with, fashion means nothing to me. It's not that I don't embrace fashion; I have no concept of what it is. I truly believe they should make Garanimals for adults, to allow me to know which shirt to match with what pants. It was quite a challenge to pick out shirts that did not make me look bald, fat, and desperate (*that is a lot to ask from a shirt*).

Finally, selected a half-dozen or so that I felt had the best shot to make me look *not-half-bad*, and headed off to the "*photo-shoot.*"

Once at my friend's apartment, we discussed the logistics as to where we should take this photograph. He suggested outside, but I did not feel comfortable with that. I couldn't help but think what his neighbors thought when they saw this six-foot-two-tall man enter the apartment with a change of wardrobe; I wasn't about to put on a fashion show for them as well. We agreed upon a relatively neutral corner of his apartment, far from any rogue reflective surfaces (*we've all seen the naked man reflect in the teapot*).

Before we began, he offered me a drink. It would have been rude of me to decline. Before any fashion show, I'm sure, everyone has a drink or two.

Or three.

Or four.

Now, well lubricated, we proceeded to the task at hand.

I don't photograph well because I don't know how to smile on cue (*yeah, that's the reason*). I thought if we made it look like a candid shot, maybe it wouldn't be too bad. My head turned back, as if someone just tapped me on the shoulder, or that surprised expression when I suddenly realize there's a man in the corner with a camera about to take my picture (*what are **you** doing here?*).

This was my Saturday—I changed shirts and positions while I tried to look thoughtfully-casually-surprised.

After we tried for an hour to get a staged, spontaneous photograph, we agreed upon the least-worst picture to put up on the profile. A shot of me from the waist up, left hand in pocket, right hand partially extended, as if I were about to ask the viewer for spare change.

Fortunately, bloodshot eyes didn't not appear in the photo.

The funny thing was, that in the end, it was all for nothing.

Fate, after it watched my sad attempt at self-portrait, stepped in and took care of the problem for me.

A few weeks later, at a family function, while I stood out on the lawn, my sister called over to me.

I turned around (*what are **you** doing here?*) and she snapped what turned out to be the best picture of me—ever. It was so good that people, upon seeing the photo, did not even recognize me. I was smiling. I was tan and fit (*not sure how that happened*), with one shoulder jauntily dipped lower than the other.

I must have reminded my sister ten times to email me that picture; I wanted it for my profile.

It went up the next day, and has been reused on every social media site that I have ever been a member of.

If I could go back in time and put it in my high school yearbook, I would.

That picture lived up to the bio I created much better than the awkward poses in my friend's apartment.

Fate is a wonderful photographer—I should ask it to do my wedding.

PLUTO, YOU WILL ALWAYS BE A PLANET TO ME

Why did we think a lecture about Pluto, at a local winery, would be a fun event on a Friday night? Oh, right—*winery*. With the lure of alcohol to draw us in (*if I was an animal, I'd be enticed into the open by a hunter with a nice glass of cabernet*) our small group found ourselves waiting for the lecture to begin.

I've always felt sorry for Pluto. Once the status of planet was removed, she deserved a much better advocate than the one we faced that night.

Then again, we didn't exactly help her case.

We found a spot near the back of the room, turned a four-chair table into an eight-chair; overstuffed, like a lifeboat with too many survivors. Bottles of wine were purchased and placed strategically. Then, like moms in a movie theater, treats and snacks were pulled from pocketbooks and scattered about.

We settled in, and were promptly treated to a technically advanced science lecture. That is, if that lecture was presented in nineteen-seventy-two, and I was in eighth grade.

In an era of wireless, high-definition electronics, we

witnessed an overhead projector, and a paper-mache model of Pluto and her moon.

It wasn't a large venue, but the lecturer spoke without a microphone. At our age, hearing is one of the first things to go, so what happened next was forgivable.

Several bottles of wine in, and some time into the lecture, most of us strained to absorb what was said by the speaker named a scientist who is associated with Pluto. The scientist's last name was Stern.

To preserve their anonymity, I will not say who, but suddenly a voice from our table yelled out, "Baba Booey! Baba Booey!"

After there was no reaction from the crowd, this person leaned toward me and asked, "He said Howard Stern, right?"

Yes, he did, because we all know that Howard Stern is a famous talk show host / astrophysicist.

It was Alan Stern.

I should mention now, we were "shushed" a few times during the evening. They were the rowdy kids in grade school who heckled from the cheap seats, but now with more alcohol.

Periodically, a glass was knocked over. At one point, my brother's sister-in-law knocked one wine bottle into another as she tried to pick up the spare.

The talk continued. Each time the lecturer passed in front of the screen, the image jumped from the white board to the front of his shirt, and then back again.

He went on to explain what makes a planet, and to illustrate he picked up his paper-mache model of Pluto and her moon. I pictured him in his basement, slathering sticky strips of paper to a balloon for the planet, and a rubber ball for the moon.

He attached the two models together with a stick. In

front of us, he spun the two objects in rotation as he moved around a wooden column, which was a stand in for the sun.

In space, no one can hear you yawn.

Apparently, Pluto is not a planet for two reasons. One, the moon and the planet rotate as one object, as demonstrated by the papier-mache ballet we just witnessed. Two, on the last day of a five-day conference somewhere in Europe, the only people who remained were the newcomers and zealots. The older members, who knew you never stay until the end of a five-day conference, were off exchanging formulas in a hotel room somewhere.

With no adult supervision, someone always gets hurt.

This time it was Pluto; she never saw it coming.

They voted her out.

As the lecture about Pluto and the planets drew to a close, he asked for questions from the audience. A woman asked a long, complicated question (*I think she was one of those that shushed us*), and I felt she was a plant.

By now, I was in the back of the room, talking to my brother's brother-in-law. The lecturer moved across the front, then said, "We have time for one more question. Yes, you in the back."

Surprised, he pointed at me, and I noticed that my hand was indeed up in the air.

"Oh, I don't have a question," I replied. "I'm Italian, this is how I talk".

We finished the wine, gathered the snacks, and made our way out to the car. We may have learned a thing or two about Pluto over the course of the last few hours, but there was one thing I definitely came away with that night.

No matter how old you are, when someone says *"Uranus,"* you are going to laugh.

LIGHTS, CAMERA, PULL OVER

There are many things that make us jump, but none so more than the red-and-blue lights of a police cruiser bursting from your rear view mirror.

Anyone who has driven with me, or behind me, knows that I drive in the right lane at speed limit or below. Once, a friend drove behind me on the highway. After a few minutes, my cell phone lit up.

"Al, is that you?" she laughed. "You drive like a turtle!"

Slow and steady wins the race.

So, the few times I was pulled over by the police, it was not for speeding.

About four years ago, the day before Christmas Eve, I dropped off supplies for a family gathering. With bad weather conditions forecast, I wanted to ensure that if I couldn't make the trip on the day of the party, my contribution would not be missed.

Afterwards, to get home, I had to take Route 31 in New Jersey. Let me preface this with: I hate Route 31. The road twists and turns so much that cars coming toward me look like they are in my lane. Now, throw in that it was twilight and an absolutely driving rain/snow storm.

In my mind, a head-on collision was imminent.

To avoid that fate, under the rain and snow and death machines flying at me, I hugged the fog-line on the highway like we were dating. Guess I squeezed a little too tight, because within seconds the red-and-blue lights beckoned me to pull over to the shoulder.

I turned on my interior lights, gathered my documents, and waited for the officer to appear by my driver's side window, which was half-open to limit the amount of water that invaded my car.

When the officer arrived I handed over my documents, then we chatted a bit. His concern was that I periodically swerved over the aforementioned fog line.

He inquired that, since it was a few days before Christmas, perhaps I was coming from a work Christmas party and maybe had a few drinks?

At this point, I have to either bluff my way through or tell him the truth.

Well, truth hurts, but here we go.

"No Christmas party, I just hate driving on this road and driving at night. I feel like the cars are driving at me, and in this weather, I prefer the fog line to the center line."

A long pause followed, then...

"OK," he handed me back the documents, "you have a good night."

So, back to the highway of death I went.

Spoiler alert: I didn't die.

Now jump to last week. Just a few miles from my house, on a two-lane back road, the car behind me exploded with red-and-blue lights, and insanely bright headlights blinded me.

On the shoulder, turned on the interior lights, lowered

the windows, and gathered my documents. The officer, now framed in my passenger door window, asked for my license, insurance, and registration, which I promptly handed to him.

He introduced himself, and informed me that I was being filmed.

That was bad, because I heard the camera adds about fifty pounds.

The officer then asked, "Do you know why I pulled you over?"

Told him no, I did not.

"Well," he continued, "you weren't speeding *(which comes as a surprise to no one)* but I noticed you swerved over the double line a few times. Where are you coming from?"

Then added, "Did you have anything to drink?"

I told him I was coming from The Rail, in Whitehouse, which is a bar/restaurant that does trivia on Wednesday nights *(maybe too much of a back story)* and that I had two glasses of red wine between 7:30 and 9:30.

In a very short time I found myself standing behind my car. The police cruiser's headlights illuminated me to cars that passed.

"First," the officer stated, "stand up straight with your feet together."

With feet together, I turned into a Weeble about to fall down. At my age, and with a blind spot in my right eye, my sense of balance has been compromised over the years, and this would be a horrible time to waver.

"Keep your head straight, and follow my pen with your eyes."

(In my head: Don't fall over, don't fall over, don't fall over.)

"Okay."

The pen in front of me moved left to center to right. I followed with my eyes, but then:

"Don't move your head."

"Sorry."

Center, left, center.

"Don't move your head."

"Sorry."

You would be surprised how hard it is, standing on the side of the road, at night, bathed in the beams of a police car, not to move your head as an officer waves a pen across your field of vision.

After a few more minutes the officer, convinced I was not drunk, told me I could leave.

Back in my car, hands firmly cast at ten and two on the wheel, I made it back to my house unscathed.

Jump to that weekend, a family event, around the kitchen table, of course I tell the story of how I was pulled over *(doesn't everyone discuss police encounters at their next family gathering?)*. Interestingly, my nephew's wife is a police detective, and she explains the reason for the side-of-the-road pen and the eyes test.

Seems that, if you are over the limit, your pupils will stutter-step as you move them left to right. There is nothing you can do to stop that. You don't even know that it is happening.

This is a Public Service Announcement.

Hopefully, in the future, no red-and-blue lights will come alive in my rear view mirror ever again.

Remember, slow and steady wins the race.

Maybe I should make a bumper sticker.

PLEASE, DON'T DRIVE OFF THE MOUNTAIN

Author's Note: *For this post, I am not using real names. I'm not hiding a crime (well, not really) and the people involved know who they are. Usually, I would ask the people in the post if I could use their names, but in this case, I don't have access to everyone, so "the names have been changed to protect...me."*

I have been in three major car accidents in my life. When I say major, I mean car(s) destroyed, ambulances called *(fire trucks for one of them)*, and people ended up in the hospital.

In chronological order, this is the second on a very short *(hopefully)* list.

In the seventies, I found myself in the second car of a two-car-caravan headed to a campsite somewhere in Pennsylvania. Never in my life did I have any desire to go camping, but there I was. Each car had four people, packed with equipment we needed for the weekend. The driver of our car, Jack *(it was his car)* followed the leader. We specifically told the driver of the first car we did not know where we were going, so please do not lose us.

They lost us three miles into the trip.

The seventies means no cells, no GPS, just a relative

knowledge of the area of the campsite; we'll figure something out.

Turned out, we didn't need to know.

Well into Pennsylvania, we weaved our way up a mountain, still not sure where we were headed, but confident we'd get there.

Oh, by the way, did I mention we were drinking?

We were drinking.

Empty beer cans filled the car floor *(we wouldn't dream of littering)*. Up into the mountain we climbed, a long drop just the other side of the guard rail.

Cars in the seventies were tanks, a great deal of space inside. So much so, I was able to turn completely in my seat, lean over the headrest, and talk to Tom and Jimmy in the back seat.

Captain Jack by *Billy Joel* was on the radio. But, in my head I thought, *"What's that other sound?"*

Then it hit me: it was the sound the tires made when they hit gravel on the shoulder of the highway. Without a thought, I gripped the headrest just as the car hit the rail, flipped over, and rolled down the side of a mountain.

As we rolled, all I saw was a tunnel of black in front of my eyes. I was a sock in the spin cycle, just waiting for the machine to buzz.

When the cycle ended, the car found itself driver's side down. I looked, and the first thing I saw was Jack, eyes closed, a red streak under his chin from ear to ear.

Opened the passenger side door and climbed up, and out, of the car. On the side of the embankment Tom sat; apparently, on the upturn, he was thrown from the car. And, oddly, it knocked the laces out of his shoes.

I continued up toward the highway. Stood on the asphalt, waved my arms for a car to stop. First car drove passed me, so I kicked the back panel, but it continued on its way.

The next car slowed enough for me to yell, "Call an ambulance—we've been in an accident!"

After that, car after car stopped. A few people climbed down to the wreck with me. Someone noticed all the beer, so a few minutes later a group of people, who didn't know each other just moments before, threw beer cans, both empty and full, into the woods.

Went back into the car and got Jack out. Jimmy climbed out the rear window, and eventually, we all ended up on the highway.

The ambulance arrived and took us to the hospital.

In the emergency room, the doctor checked us over. Fortunately, Jack's neck wound was superficial, and Jimmy had a cut on his arm. After the doctor heard the account of the accident, he stated that it could have been much worse, and we were extremely lucky.

Jack *(the diver)*, after he heard the doctor's comment, and after he rolled his car off a mountain, chimed in:

"Yeah, and if my grandmother had balls, she'd be my grandfather."

(He absolutely said that.)

By the way, the doctor was closer to the truth than he knew *(it could have been much, much worse)*.

Where we went over the rail, the roll down the grade was about two-stories long. However, if we had gone over the rail a few miles back, it was a sheer drop; they never would have found us, or the car.

By the end of the day, Jack and Jimmy were admitted to the hospital for their injuries; Tom and I were let go.

In a town that rolled up its sidewalks at 8 pm, we were lucky to find a small hotel *(think Shady Rest),* and something to eat.

The next morning, I felt like I'd been hit by a truck. Took all my energy to get out of bed and shower. My body never hurt this much, every move a challenge. Tom was the same way.

Two decrepit twenty-somethings inched their way toward the hospital. When we got there, two idiots hung out the hospital window, waved and yelled good morning to us.

Guess a night in a hospital does wonders after a car accident, as opposed to a night in an old, run down hotel.

Who knew?

Went to the junkyard where they brought the car. We walked around for a good half-hour trying to find it. When we couldn't find it, we gathered to think what to do next. It was only then we realized we were standing right in front of it. That's how damaged the car was; didn't even recognize it.

The way it looked, you'd think no one got out alive.

We retrieved our luggage and equipment, but we were still far from home.

Next step: call the Pennsylvania State Police, give our friends' names and campsite to inform them what happened and to come and get us.

Two cars, eight people, filled with equipment left New Jersey less than twenty-four-hours ago. Now, within an hour of calling our friends, one car, eight people, filled with equipment, left Pennsylvania to go home. Without a doubt, the worst car ride in the history of car rides. I think my liver still has the impression of the armrest jammed into my side the entire way home.

So, what lessons have we learned from all this?

Do not drink and drive.

And, for the love of god, please, don't drive off the mountain.

THE TIME I ALMOST DIED LIKE A ROCK STAR

No one wants to die in a stupid way. You know, something that will end up a punch line of their life once they are gone. Preferably, I would like to die in my sleep and, one night a few years ago, I almost got my wish.

Most people my age sleep alludes. Unfortunately, it's not my age that keeps me awake at night. I have been that way for as long as I remember. The irony about that is for years, at any point of the day, I could roll over on the couch and fall asleep in an instant.

"Nothing good on TV, I think I'll take a nap."

Off to dreamland.

But night was another story *(well, this story, actually)*.

Eventually, I found a method that would help me sleep at night. Although, sleep may not be the best description of how my time passed. The least healthy method I chose?

Scotch.

When the day was done, a few glasses of scotch on the rocks, and off to the land of Morpheus I'd go.

Now, you are thinking I should have tried a white noise machine *(which I tried—did not work)*, soothing music *(nope)*,

TV in the background *(again, nope)* or any other dozens of internet searched methods to fall asleep.

Nothing worked.

Scotch? Yes, that worked. Maybe not the best method, but it got me from midnight to morning.

Over time, I knew that this was not the best way to find sleep. My brother told me that red wine would be good for me, and that it would help me get to sleep. So, I tried it.

A step in the right direction, but not quite there.

Then I found the missing piece to the sleep puzzle.

But before I reveal that, I know that all I have written above and about to write below is incredibly bad for me.

The missing piece?

ZzzQuil.

Yes, *ZzzQuil*, the nighttime cold medications from VICKS. *(Note: this is not a recommendation or a condemnation of the product.)*

The combination of two glasses of red wine and the measured dose of *ZzzQuil* turned out to be the magic potion.

It worked for a while but, unfortunately for me, I missed my scotch. So, after several weeks, I went back to my original routine of scotch and a fitful sleep.

Then, one night, as I headed into the early morning of the next day, the scotch not doing it's job, I had an idea.

After I already drank a good amount of scotch, I followed that up with a measured dose of ZzzQuil.

Surprisingly, it worked.

Unfortunately, maybe too well.

When my alarm went off in the morning, I did not respond. When it went off a second, third, fourth time, I did not respond. Finally, shaken from my slumber, I hit the snooze button and reached for my phone. Not sure of the time, I called my friend Bill, whom I worked with at the time, to tell him I needed a vacation day. When he inquired if something was wrong, I simply grunted and ended the call.

My head in a fog, bags of cement lay on my chest, I could not move.

For hours, I slipped in and out of consciousness *(not sleep; this was not sleep)* until my eyes stayed open for more than five minutes. Rolled over, and surprised by the time on the clock —it was two-thirty in the afternoon.

More than twelve hours in this self-induced limbo.

"For in this sleep of death what dreams may come..."

I'm no rock star, and definitely no Hamlet, so, in the end, I just went back to scotch and bad, fitful nights where sleep, apparently, is an afterthought.

Rock on.

A LONG OVERDUE SALUTE TO THE COLONEL

Recently, I received a friend request on Facebook from a woman whose name I did not recognize.

She then sent me a message that she worked with me at the Colonel's Garter (*trust me, it's a name of a bar name from the eighties*) and I immediately accepted. You don't ignore a voice from the past.

After a short text message exchange, I thought about my time in that job. Made me think, *"I should write about this"*.

So, Carol, thank you for the inspiration; this is for you.

Author's Note: *What follows is my memory, it may be right, it may be wrong, but it's mine. In addition, I may not use names for two reasons:*

One: to protect someone's anonymity.

Two: I just don't remember their names.

In the late seventies, early eighties, there were a string of bars that peppered New Jersey. They all began with the name Art Stock's (*insert name of bar here*).

Art Stock, as far as I knew, was a school teacher that somehow became the "name" of a series of bars in the state. I worked in two "Art Stock" bars, the Royal Manor North, and the Colonel's Garter.

By far, the better bar was the Colonel's Garter.

To be clear, I was a bouncer, not a bartender. Worked the door, roamed the floor, stood by the stage while the band played *(maybe that's why I have lousy hearing)*. It was a very casual atmosphere. For instance, even though the drinking age was still eighteen, sometimes patrons would enter who "forget their IDs."

My reply?

"Just open your wallet," I would say. "Show me something. A picture of your dog, your favorite Aunt, I don't care. Just show me something."

To which they would, and I'd let them in.

Air Guitar was big back in the early eighties. For those unenlightened, basically you stood on stage while a song played, and mimicked playing a guitar. Each week, The Garter *(as we called it)* had an air guitar contest. Some would get into it, jump up and down on the stage, one arm circling the imaginary instrument.

However, that was nothing compared to what a friend I'd known since high school did one night.

He walked up on stage, the music started, and he played air guitar. When the song ended, he took a bow, then pulled up his shirt, pulled down his pants *(and underwear)* and raised his arms in triumph.

During this display, my manager, Ray, stood next to me on the floor. He laughed, then asked, "Isn't that your friend?"

"Yes," I tentatively replied.

"Well, tell him he's banned for a month."

Exactly one month later, with the ban lifted, my friend went up on stage—and did it again.

To my knowledge, after the second ban from the club, he retired his air guitar act.

There is a slight addendum to his action. During his "act" he started a chant about a body part (one which everyone could clearly see), but I can not, and will not, repeat it here.

Just know, there was chanting.

The best part of working in a bar, also the worst, was closing time. It is so hard to get drunks to leave a bar when the lights come on. Around and around I'd go, tell people to leave, and they just didn't get the hint. In reality, we just wanted them out so the staff could drink while the band of the night broke down their equipment. While the band did that, we'd drink for free and play video games *(usually PAC-Man and Ms. PAC-Man—don't judge us, it was the eighties)*.

Sometimes, we didn't leave the bar until the sun peered over the horizon.

Did you know, when bartenders cleaned their stations, they would serve us a drink called a "Jim Jones?"

What is a "Jim Jones?" Glad you asked.

Quick history lesson: Jim Jones was a cult leader that killed his followers with a lethal concoction of cyanide and fruit juice. It's where the phrase "Drink the Kool-Aid" comes from.

For us, it was a concoction of all the alcohol run-off collected in the rubber mats underneath where the bartenders mixed their drinks *(vodka, gin, tequila, scotch, mixers, soda, etc)*. We would end up doing shots of this conglomerate of liquids *(amazed we are still alive)*.

During one of these after-hours meetings, my manager, Ray, said to me, "Al, before I hired you," he laughed, "I would order one case of Tanqueray every three months. Now, it's a case a month."

My drink of choice during work hours? Tanqueray and club soda.

I think it was just a coincidence.

It wasn't all just business, of course. There were also affairs of the heart.

Well, almost.

There was a woman that worked at the Imported Beer Bar that I liked. Back then, it didn't take much for me to like a woman, but it took me to move a mountain to actually tell her.

I did, I asked her out, and she said yes *(cue the fireworks montage)*.

The next night, as I walked into work, this woman came out to meet me in the parking lot. How sweet was that? Here she was, greeting me before work started.

Turns out, not so sweet.

She came out to tell that she could not go out with me because she liked someone else.

Side Note: *It's always High School.*

I guess *(actually, I know),* that I don't handle rejection well. The rest of the night was a drunken blur, and because we took care of each other during trying times *(well, I'd find out later what might have happened during these "trying times")* I was given a ride home.

The next night, when I made it back to work, I was told that there was a discussion, with me in my inebriated state, they wanted to put me on a plane to Boston, as a joke *(this was the eighties; you could actually do that).*

But, instead, they drove me home.

I'd like to thank those that voted against this absolutely horrible idea, because I don't think I would have done well, drunk and alone in Boston *(new reality show?).*

When it was over, and the bar was sold, the new owner decided that what South Amboy needed was a New York City-style Night Club *(it did not).*

On the last night of the Colonel's Garter, the band Flossie

played. Flossie was the lead singer and she wore tight red leather pants.

Pure rock'n'roll.

The night the new re-imaged bar opened *(City Lights)*, and was now like a New York Night Club, Flossie *(also re-imaged)* stepped out on stage in an evening gown.

Neither the bar, nor the band, worked.

A few years later, the bar became a strip-club called "Delilah's Den."

After that, who knows if the building still exists, but all I know is...

...well, it was fun while it lasted.

...AND ONE MORE FOR THE ROAD

I grew up at a time that drunk driving was encouraged *(kidding, of course— sort of)*. By that, I mean, whenever we were pulled over, and the driver was obviously drinking *(first clue: there were open beers in the car)* the officer(s) would confiscate our remaining beers, and told us to go home.

One night, a day or so after New Years, we'd just left *Pete's (a bar where if you could see over the top of the bar, you could get served)*.

When we left the bar, some took their unfinished beers with them *(still in their respective glasses)* and headed to the next bar *("The Bottle Stop" in South Amboy)*.

Driving on Route Five-sixteen *(ironically, right by the high school)*, the unwanted glow of police lights filled the car.

Immediately, I pulled over, and as I searched for my documents, I noticed Billy in the back seat, full beer still in his hand.

"Billy," I demanded, "get rid of that beer!"

"OK," he replied, then guzzled the remaining beer just as the officer walked past the back passenger window.

What should have followed was an array of tickets issued, car impounded, and loss of my license.

But, remember, this was the Renaissance of drunk driving.

I was told to drop everyone off, and go home. To tell you the truth, I don't remember if that's what I did, but odds are, I didn't.

Another time, my friend Chris and I headed down the shore after the bars closed to just look at the ocean (*we did that stuff back then*). A straight run, Route Eighteen to Thirty-four and straight into Asbury Park.

On Route Thirty-four, once again, from out of the darkness, red-and-blue lights filled my car. I pulled over, looked for my documents, and waited. After the police officer reviewed my license, registration, and insurance he asked us to step out of the car.

As we stood on the shoulder he went through my car, back seat, front seat, and when he pulled several beer cans from under the passenger seat (*some empty, some full*), we thought that was it.

However, to our utter surprise, he just continued to search the car.

With great trepidation I asked the officer, "What are you looking for?"

Without hesitation he said, "Drugs," and continued his search.

Chris and I, who knew full well there was nothing in the car, stepped back and smiled.

When no drugs were found, we found ourselves back on the road to Asbury Park.

(*OK, this is the best part.*)

On our way back home, after we saw the ocean (*again, for no reason except it's what we did*), we passed that same police car on the side of the road. In my rear view, I saw him start to pull out to chase us, when, I assume, he recognized us from the previous stop. So, instead of following us, he flashed his brights as an acknowledgment, then rolled back into his spot to wait for the next "drug dealer" to cross his path.

With the above said, don't drink and drive. We may have gotten away with a lot when my friends and I were younger, but I also hit a telephone pole going forty-miles-an-hour. Was very lucky, as was the aforementioned friend, Chris *(maybe Chris should have stopped driving with me)* to walk away with just stitches and bruises.

We had fun, but remember, don't drink and drive.

Oh, and, don't do drugs.

ABOUT THE AUTHOR

Al DeLuise is a retired computer programmer by day, a scotch drinker by night, and a divorced, balding father of three all the time. Now that his kids are too old to live at home but not too old to quit asking him for money, he spends his time adding to his Netflix queue, looking for love in many (if not all) of the wrong places, and going to his ex-wife's house for dinner.

Made in the USA
Middletown, DE
07 January 2024

47377686R00054